YOUR KNOWLEDGE HAS VALUE

- We will publish your bachelor's and master's thesis, essays and papers

- Your own eBook and book - sold worldwide in all relevant shops

- Earn money with each sale

Upload your text at www.GRIN.com and publish for free

Can annexation be justified? Analysing Russia's annexation of Crimea

Jonathan Rößler

Bibliographic information published by the German National Library:

The German National Library lists this publication in the National Bibliography; detailed bibliographic data are available on the Internet at http://dnb.dnb.de.

ISBN: 9783668491106
This book is also available as an ebook.

Print and binding: Books on Demand GmbH, Norderstedt, Germany
Printed on acid-free paper from responsible sources.

The present work has been carefully prepared. Nevertheless, authors and publishers do not incur liability for the correctness of information, notes, links and advice as well as any printing errors.

GRIN web shop: https://www.grin.com/document/369393

Can annexation be justified?

Analysing Russia's annexation of Crimea.

Summer Term 2017

University of Birmingham

Department of Political Science and International Studies

Essay

by

Jonathan Rößler

for

"Law, Politics and the International System"

Can annexation be justified?

Introduction

Crimea's unilateral secession and subsequent accession to Russia was certainly one of the most conflictual and consequential cases in recent international law and politics. This essay, therefore, seeks to give an answer to the question if and how annexation can be justified and whether this was the case with Crimea.

The prohibition and unlawfulness of annexation by invasion is an established norm in international law and normative scholarship. It was already established in the League of Nations covenant and is today enshrined in Art. 2 (4) of the United Nations (UN) Charter which states that "All Members shall refrain [...] from the threat or use of force against the territorial integrity or political independence of any state [...]" (United Nations General Assembly (UNGA), 1945). Accordingly, a possibly justified annexation is only imaginable if it comes to a peaceful legal agreement between the entity that wishes to be annexed and the annexing state. Such a treaty of incorporation would entail the transfer of full competence in respect of the territory being annexed (Grant, 2015: 71). Hence, the crucial question in regard to the justification of annexation is whether the entity that wishes to become part of another state has the competence to conclude such a treaty. A possibly legitimate annexation must consequently be understood as a two-step process, consisting of firstly, the secession of an entity from its parent state and secondly, the incorporation of this newly emerged state into a third state's territory. Annexation becomes thus a process of secession that consummates in the form of integration with another state (Vidmar, 2015: 366).

For this reason, this essay will start providing an insight into two different academic theories of secession to shed light on the question if and when secession can be justified from a normative point of view. Rather than coming to a definite conclusion, this part seeks to outline the current theoretical debate on secession. Afterwards, the contemporary state of international law and state practice on secession will be examined. Finally, the secession and Russia's subsequent annexation of Crimea, as well as the reaction of the international community, will be analysed. This essay comes to the conclusion that although secession and subsequent annexation can theoretically be justified, this was not the case with Crimea.

Theories of Secession

There are two categories of normative[1] theories of secession. The first type is called primary-right, the second remedial-right-only. Both categories lie between the poles of two moral rights: Firstly, the people's inherent right to self-determination[2] and secondly, the state's right to territorial integrity[3]. According to Buchanan, the latter derives its moral legitimacy from the state's population's inherent rights on protection and participation (Buchanan, 1997: 49).

Primary-right theories construe the notion of self-determination widely and assume that a right to secession exist even from a state that is perfectly just. However, the question who the bearer of this right would be remains highly controversial (Buchanan, 1997: 41). It is worth noting that even the comparatively loose primary-right theories set some conditions for secession, for example, that the new state must be viable and must respect the human rights of its population (Catala, 2015, 686).

In contrast, the more restrictive remedial-right-only theories assume that a right to secede exist solely if a group has suffered certain injustices for which secession is the appropriate remedy. Remedial-right-only theories draw upon the Lockean idea that the people have a legitimate right to overthrow a government when it violates their fundamental rights. This means that secession may be justified and feasible as a response of last resort to "selective tyranny, when revolution is not a practical prospect" (Buchanan, 1997: 36).

International Law and State Practice

Although international law neither explicitly prohibits, nor encourages secession, state practice strongly favours the continuity and territorial integrity of states; cases of decolonization are the only exceptions.[4] The normal situation after a unilateral declaration of independence is that the predecessor state will continue in existence and be recognised as such (Crawford, 1999: 93). Besides the case of Bangladesh, which must rather be seen as an Indian *fait accompli* that was subsequently accepted by Pakistan (Fisch, 2010: 240; Crawford, 2006: 141), no non-colonial unilateral secession was successful in the 20th century. The only successful and certainly the most controversial unilateral secession in the 21st century was the one of Kosovo in 2008. However, because of its unique history and the rather vacuous evaluation of the International Court of Justice (ICJ) regarding the legal base of the

---

[1] "Normative" understood here as opposite to "explanatory".
[2] As articled in Art. 1(2) UN Charter.
[3] Established, for example, in Art. 5(7) of the "Friendly-Relations-Declaration" (UNGA, 1970).
[4] For this aspect, see Crawford (1999: 87-92).

secession[5], Kosovo's declaration of independence was widely regarded as a case *sui generis* (Heintze, 2014: 135). The widespread view that Kosovo did not provide a precedent is illustrated by the following statement of the Independent International Fact-Finding Mission on the Conflict in Georgia (IIFFMCG) which also sums up the stance of international law on secession and self-determination:

> *"[Outside] the colonial context, self-determination is basically limited to internal self-determination. A right to self-determination in form of secession is not accepted in state practice. A limited conditional extraordinary allowance to secede as a last resort in extreme cases is debated in international legal scholarship. However, most authors opine that such a remedial "right" or allowance does not form part of international law as it stands. The case of Kosovo has not changed the rules"* (IIFFMCG, 2009: 141).

A case of unilateral declaration of independence becomes especially explosive when the exercise of self-determination connects to the use of force. Crawford states that in regard to such a case, "[an] entity claiming statehood but created during a period of foreign military occupation will be presumed not to be independent" (Crawford, 2006: 148) and that "[an] entity created in violation of the rules relating to the use of force [...] will not be regarded as a state" (ibid.). In the next part of this essay, the legality of Crimea's secession and annexation will be assessed.

Crimea

The legality of Crimea's secession and annexation will be examined under consideration of the previous theoretical inquiries and structured by the following four questions: 1. Was Crimea a case of remedial secession? 2. Was the referendum a valid act of self-determination? 3. What impact did Russia's interference have on the legitimacy of the secession? 4. Can an illegal annexation be healed by recognition?

Was Crimea a case of remedial secession?

To its unilateral secession being legal, Crimea's right to self-determination would have needed to entail a right to secede. As shown earlier, the very existence of such a right is

---

[5] As expressed by Judge Yusuf in a separate opinion, the ICJ failed to cease the opportunity to define the scope and normative content of a postcolonial right of self-determination (ICJ, 2010: 16).

controversially debated in international legal scholarship and basically non-existent in state practice. However, if Crimea would have been a case of remedial secession, it could have been justified at least from a moral, though perhaps not legal, perspective.

Russia claims that the conditions of the Russian ethnic population in Crimea supported the exercise of self-determination by means of remedial secession (Grant, 2015: 73). Yet, this was hardly the case. The Office of the High Commissioner for Human Rights (OHCHR) stated that the alleged human right violations of ethnic Russians were "neither systemic nor widespread" (OHCHR, 2014: 4). The high commissioner on national minorities of the Organisation for Security and Co-operation in Europe (OSCE) reported no human rights problems concerning Crimea's ethnic Russian population after her visit of Crimea in March 2014 (Thors, 2014) and instead of referring to ethnic Russians, the United Nations Human Rights Council (HRC) was in recent years rather concerned about the situation of the Crimean Tatars (HRC, 2008). Russia's claim that a crisis had erupted in February 2014 in which the Russian population of Crimea was in peril was shared by no other international actor (Grant, 2015: 75).

The unanimous juridical opinion is that if a right to remedial secession would exist, it could only be an "ultima ratio" (Marxsen, 2014: 386), a last resort to solve a crisis after the exhaustion of all other means (Buchanan, 1997: 36), limited to "the most extreme of cases" (Canadian Supreme Court, 1998). However, neither the threshold of oppression nor the definition of a remedy of last resort had been met in Crimea (Vidmar, 2015: 372). Thus, in contrast to Bangladesh or Kosovo, where severe crimes against humanity have occurred, Crimea can certainly not be considered a case of remedial secession even if one takes the most-far reaching suggestions for such a right (Marxsen, 2014: 387).

Was the referendum a valid act of self-determination?
With a right to remedial secession clearly being denied in the Crimean case, there is no legal justification for Crimea's unilateral secession feasible under international law. A referendum, being a necessary but not sufficient condition for secession, does not create a right to secession either. Consequently, the outcome of the referendum is, at least legally, irrelevant. Nevertheless, it is important to take a look at the validity of the referendum as the Russian pro-annexation argumentation builds strongly on it.

Even in the context of decolonization where a unilateral right to secession exists, certain procedural conditions apply when conducting an act of self-determination (Grant, 2015: 76).

The UNGA states that such an act must be "the result of a free and voluntary choice by the people of the territory concerned expressed through informed and democratic process" (UNGA, 1960: Annex). State practice, for example, the Canadian "Clarity Act", further suggests that the question asked must be unambiguous and that the act must reflect a real choice (Grant, 2015: 76). These procedural safeguards that apply to colonial cases, seem to apply *a fortiori* in cases where the existence of a right to secession is at least contested (op. cit. 77).

In Crimea, the referendum of independence was neither overseen by the UN nor did it satisfy basic regional standards for the conduct of popular consultations (ibid.). Additionally, the two possible answers provided were at least ambiguous. Firstly, because the status quo was not even offered. Secondly, because restoring the 1992 constitution (the only given alternative to a unification with Russia) meant that Crimea would have become an independent unit within Ukraine but with a broad right to self-determination, including a possible unification with Russia. Thus, "[effectively], the choice may well have been between straightforward integration with Russia and a somewhat complicated integration with Russia" (Vidmar, 2015: 381). Therefore, the referendum failed the most basic requirements applied to an act of self-determination, undermining its moral validity. Moreover, the validity of the referendum was compromised by its timing. Crimea's secession was conducted without any preceding negotiations with the Ukrainian government and under presence of presumably Russian military forces. The legal impact of the latter will be examined in the following.

What impact did Russia's interference have on the legitimacy of the secession?
Russia justified its military intervention, which followed the referendum, with several legal arguments ranging from "intervention by invitation" to "humanitarian intervention". Instead of analysing Russia's justifications for its military intervention[6], this part of the essay will focus on the question which impact Russia's military presence did have on the legality of Crimea's secession.

As shown earlier, an entity created under violation of the prohibition of force cannot be regarded as a state (Crawford, 2006: 148). That even the mere unilateral declaration of independence can be illegal under violent circumstances was confirmed by the ICJ's advisory opinion on Kosovo (ICJ, 2010). The ICJ has established that no right to self-determination can apply when declarations of independence are accompanied by unlawful threat or use of

---

[6] For this, see Allison (2014).

force and thus the violation of peremptory international law (Allison 2014, 1266). The crucial question is therefore whether Russia violated any *jus cogens* in regard to Crimea's secession. Immediately after Yanukovych's overthrow, pro-Russian militias took over control of Crimea and initiated the process of secession and accession to Russia (Marxsen, 2015: 369). After the Russian Council authorised the use of armed forces on the territory of Ukraine on the 1st of March 2014, Russian forces in Crimea were reinforced and gathered at the Ukrainian border (ibid.). Although Russia proclaimed that the unmarked forces that acted in Crimea prior to the referendum were Crimean self-defence units, the evidence strongly suggest that Russian troops played an important role in taking over Crimean infrastructure and blocking Ukrainian military units (op. cit. 370). Hence, already before the referendum Russia presumably violated the prohibition of force and certainly violated the prohibition of threat of force (Vidmar, 2015: 382). After the referendum, an open Russian military intervention took place. Leaving aside the question of whether this was justified or not, its mere conduct had serious implications for the legal status of Crimea: In the absence of a widespread international recognition of the referendum, Crimea's referendum and independence would have remained ineffective without Russia's forceful intervention (Krisch, 2014). Hence, comparable to the case of Northern Cyprus, Russia used military force to make Crimea's secession effective (Vidmar, 2015: 367). With this, Russia created an illegal territorial situation (Allison, 2014: 1266) and thus rendered Crimea's already questionable referendum and eventually its secession ultimately illegal. Crimea's subsequent accession to Russia was consequently illegal after the principle of *ex injuria jus non oritur* and perpetuated the preceding illegal violation of Ukraine's territorial integrity.

Can an illegal annexation be healed by recognition?

The previous considerations have shown that the unilateral secession of Crimea was at first at least questionable and with Russia's interference eventually clearly illegal. As Crimea has consequently not become a state, it could not enter into any treaty relations about territorial changes with Russia. Its accession to Russia is therefore without any legal effect under international law (Marxsen, 2015: 390). Consequently, the last question that will be elucidated is whether or not an illegal secession, respectively annexation, can be healed by the recognition of other states. As Crawford shows, it is theoretically possible that the effectiveness of an entity which emerged out of an illegal secession outweighs its illegal origin and that it will be recognised as a state (Crawford, 2006: 140). However, this is generally unlikely to happen because of the principle of non-recognition. This principle is articulated in the "Friendly-Relations-Declaration" which states that "no territorial acquisition resulting from the threat or use of force shall be recognised as legal" (UNGA, 1970: 6). It was affirmed by the ICJ (ICJ, 1986: 100) and the International Law Commission (ILC) which attributed it to state-responsibility (ILC, 2001: 114). Descending from the so called "Stimson-Doctrine" which referred to the non-recognition of Japan's annexation of Manchuria in 1932, the principle of non-recognition became an important customary rule of international law after the Soviet Union's annexation of the Baltic States (Hough, 1985: 481). The obligation is a powerful legal tool and aims at preventing that a *de-facto* situation that emerged under violation of peremptory norms becomes accepted in international law (Heintze, 2014: 137). As shown above, Crimea's secession and subsequent annexation were conducted in violation of *jus cogens*. This gives rise to an obligation to the international community to neither recognise Crimea's independence, nor its accession to Russia (Marxsen, 2015: 391). Hence, UNGA Resolution A/RES/68/262, adopted in March 2014, called upon all states "not to recognise any alteration of the status of the Autonomous Republic of Crimea" (UNGA, 2014: 2).

Conclusion

This essay has shown that annexation can be justified only under narrow circumstances. These are at first the implementation of a legal secession and afterwards the conduct of a bilateral treaty between the newly emerged and another state about the incorporation of the former's territory into the latter's. These conditions have not been met in the case of Crimea: Firstly, even if such a right would exist outside of the colonial context, Crimea would have surely not had a right to remedial secession. Secondly, besides the fact that a referendum cannot create a right to secede, the Crimean referendum of independence did not even meet the basic standards usually applied to acts of self-determination. Thirdly, Russia's supposed military presence before the referendum compromised the latter's validity. Russia's intervention after the referendum violated Ukraine's territorial integrity and thus made Crimea's unilateral secession ultimately illegal. Fourthly, due to the principle of non-recognition, the illegality of Crimea's annexation was certainly not healed by wide recognition.

Bibliography

Allison, R. (2014). Russian "deniable" intervention in Ukraine: how and why Russia broke the rules. *International Affairs*. Vol. 90 (6), pp. 1255-1297.

Buchanan, A. (1997). Theories of Secession. *Philosophy and Public Affairs*. Vol. 26 (1), pp. 31-61.

Canadian Supreme Court (1998). Reference re Secession of Quebec. *Report Number: 2 SCR 217, Case 25506*. URL: https://scc-csc.lexum.com/scc-csc/scc-csc/en/item/1643/index.do [Accessed 22.03.2017].

Catala, A. (2015). Secession and Annexation: The Case of Crimea. *German Law Journal*. Vol. 16 (3), pp. 581-607.

Crawford, J. (1999). State Practice and International Law in Relation to Secession. *British Yearbook of International Law*. Vol. 69 (1), pp. 85-117.

Crawford, J. (2006). *The Creation of States in International Law*. Oxford: Oxford University Press.

Fisch, J. (2010). *Das Selbstbestimmungsrecht der Völker: Die Domestizierung einer Illusion*. München: C.H. Beck.

Grant, T. (2015). Annexation of Crimea. *The American Journal of International Law*. Vol. 109 (1), pp. 68-95.

Heintze, H. (2014). Völkerrecht und Sezession – Ist die Annexion der Krim eine zulässige Wiedergutmachung sowjetischen Unrechts? *Humanitäres Völkerrecht – Informationszeitschriften*. Vol. 3, pp. 129-138.

Hough, W. (1985). The annexation of the Baltic states and its effect on the development of law prohibiting forcible seizure of territory. *New York Law School Journal of International and Comparative Law*. Vol. 6 (2), pp. 301-533.

Independent International Fact-Finding Mission on the Conflict in Georgia (2009). *Report Volume II*. URL: *http://www.mpil.de/files/pdf4/IIFFMCG_Volume_III.pdf* [Accessed 21.03.2017].

International Court of Justice (1986). Case Concerning Military and Paramilitary Activities in and Against Nicaragua. *I.C.J. Reports 1986*, p. 14-150.

International Court of Justice (2010). Accordance with international law of the unilateral declaration of independence in respect of Kosovo. *Summary 2010/2*. URL: http://www.icj-cij.org/docket/files/141/16010.pdf [Accessed 21.03.2017].

International Law Commission (2001). Report of the International Law Commission on the work of its fifty-third session. *A/56/10*.

Krisch, N. (2014). Crimea and the Limits of International Law. *EJIL: Talk!* URL: https://www.ejiltalk.org/crimea-and-the-limits-of-international-law/ [Accessed 22.03.2017].

Marxsen, C. (2014). The Crimea Crisis: An International Law Perspective. *Zeitschrift für ausländisches öffentliches Recht und Völkerrecht.* Vol. 74, pp. 367-391.

The Office of the United Nations High Commissioner for Human Rights (2014). Report of the United Nations High Commissioner for Human Rights on the situation of human rights in Ukraine. *A/HRC/27/75.*

Thors, A. (2014). Statement by the OSCE High Commissioner on National Minorities on her recent visits to Ukraine. *OSCE Press Statement.* URL: http://www.osce.org/hcnm/117175 [Accessed 22.03.2017].

United Nations General Assembly (1945). Charter of the United Nations and Statute of the International Court of Justice. New York: United Nations, Office of Public Information.

United Nations General Assembly (1960). Principles which should guide Members in determining whether or not an obligation exists to transmit the information called for under Article 73 e of the Charter. *A/RES/1541(XV).*

United Nations General Assembly (1970). Declaration on Principles of International Law Concerning Friendly Relations and Co-Operation Among States in Accordance with the Charter of the United Nations. *A/RES/25/2625.*

United Nations General Assembly (2014). Territorial Integrity of Ukraine. *A/RES/68/262.*

United Nations Human Rights Council (2008). Universal Periodic Review. Report of the Working Group on the Universal Periodic Review: Ukraine. *A/HRC/8/45.*

Vidmar, J. (2015). The Annexation of Crimea and the Boundaries of the Will of the People. *German Law Journal.* Vol. 16 (3), pp. 365-383.

YOUR KNOWLEDGE HAS VALUE

- We will publish your bachelor's and master's thesis, essays and papers

- Your own eBook and book - sold worldwide in all relevant shops

- Earn money with each sale

Upload your text at www.GRIN.com
and publish for free